THE GHOSTLY TALES OF

THE QUEEN MARY

Published by Arcadia Children's Books
A Division of Arcadia Publishing
Charleston, SC
www.arcadiapublishing.com

Spooky America is a trademark of Arcadia Publishing, Inc.

First published 2020

Manufactured in the United States

ISBN 978-1-4671-9801-1

Library of Congress Control Number: 2020938916

Notice: The information in this book is true and complete to the best of our knowledge. It is offered without guarantee on the part of the author or Arcadia Publishing. The author and Arcadia Publishing disclaim all liability in connection with the use of this book.

Photo credits: used throughout Elegant Solution/Shutterstock.com, Zhenyakot/ Shutterstock.com; p. iv-v Caso Alfonso/Shutterstock.com, Ivakoleva/Shutterstock.com, vectorkuro/Shutterstock.com, Nataliia K/Shutterstock.com, In-Finity/Shutterstock. com; p. iv-v, 98-99 Sensay/Shutterstock.com; p. vi, 46, 72 Harun Ozmen/Shutterstock. com; p. 2-3, 103 Katerina Kalugina/Shutterstock.com; p. 4, 50, 78 Rafael Trafaniuc/ Shutterstock.com; p. 12 Sloth Astronaut/Shutterstock.com; p. 16, 54, 86 Francesco Ferrarini/Shutterstock.com; p. 24, 58 Julija Sh/Shutterstock.com; p. 28-29 vectortatu/ Shutterstock.com; p. 32, 64 Maizy M/Shutterstock.com; p. 40, 68 80's Child/ Shutterstock.com; p. 83 blackstroke/Shutterstock.com.

Spooky America

THE GHOSTLY TALES OF

THE
QUEEN
MARY

SHELLI TIMMONS

Adapted from *Ghosts of the* Queen Mary, by Brian Clune with Bob Davis

ARCADIA
PUBLISHING

QUEEN MARY SHIP PLANS

SPORTS DECK 1 1 4 5 12

SUN DECK

1 4 11 3 PROMENADE DECK 9

M- DECK

A- DECK 7

B- DECK 15 3 16

13 18 2 8 R- DECK 12 14

6 2 3 17 D- DECK 10 1 2 3

Table of Contents & Map Key

Introduction

The RMS *Queen Mary* is a glorious ship, with a glorious history. She is currently a floating hotel permanently docked in Long Beach, California, welcoming guests and vacationers from around the world. As one of the most beautiful luxury ocean liners every built, lots of people come to see her grandeur and learn her history. But even more people come for something else. They come for the ghosts.

Yes, ghosts. The *Queen Mary* is a very, very haunted ship. And it's no wonder: she was first a luxury liner, then a warship, then back to a luxury liner, and now a magnificent hotel. She's seen her fair share of world leaders, dignitaries, soldiers, passengers, and crew—some who've

perished aboard and others who've decided to come visit, long after they've died. The *Queen Mary* has stories to tell. So. Many. Stories.

But before we get to the ghosts, let's get a glimpse of this incredible ship's past.

From Ocean Liner to Ghost Ship

In Scotland in 1930, the British steamship company Cunard hired John Brown & Company Shipbuilders to build a groundbreaking ship. This ship was designed to carry passengers in luxury, like today's cruise ships. But not all the passengers back then were on vacation.

And it appears not all the passengers aboard today are among the living . . . but let's not get ahead of ourselves.

Passenger ships in 1930 were much simpler than today's cruise ships. Travel by airplane was not common yet, so when people needed to travel long distances across water, they went by boat. So what made this new ship so special? It had glorious modern features, including two swimming pools, a music studio, and elevators. It would be more than fifty years before cell phones were introduced, but this ship was so advanced, it already included wireless telegraphy services. This allowed the crew to make phone calls from the middle of the ocean. It was designed to be incredibly fast for a ship of its size.

Some of the greatest artists of the time were hired to create paintings and carve the woodwork. Everything was state of the art and beautiful. One might even say hauntingly beautiful . . .

Work on the ship got off to a great start,

but it had to be stopped completely for almost three years. It was an expensive ship to build, and a global financial crisis called the Great Depression had caused problems for everyone around the world. Still eager to have the fastest, best ship on the Atlantic, the British government stepped in and provided the money to get construction going again.

On May 27, 1936, the RMS *Queen Mary* sailed her maiden voyage. It was clear she had been worth the wait. She was spectacular. Her passengers included politicians, movie stars, and royalty, as well as regular folks.

The *Queen Mary* offered tickets at three different class rates, or prices. The third-class rate was affordable for many people who wanted to come to America but were not wealthy. Fit for royalty, this ship also proudly carried immigrants into New York Harbor.

She was also very fast. She won the Blue

Riband that summer and again in 1938. (That's a fancy award for being the fastest passenger ship to cross the Atlantic.) She held the title until 1952. But then, on September 4, 1939, three days after Germany invaded Poland to kick off World War II, the RMS *Queen Mary* docked in New York Harbor and was told to stay put. It was too dangerous for her to continue sailing across the Atlantic with civilian passengers. It was time for a major change.

RMS stands for Royal Mail Service, and every RMS ship was part of the Royal Navy's fleet and yes, carried British mail. So the *Queen Mary* had always been a part of the Royal Navy. But now she was being called up for duty.

The ship was painted solid gray on the outside, and her fine furniture and artwork were removed. She was transformed to carry troops. Bunks and defense weapons were installed. From New York, she sailed to Australia, where more military equipment and medical facilities were added. Every single section of the ship was redone to carry troops. During the war, she earned a new nickname: the "Gray Ghost."

No, no, she didn't get the nickname because there were ghosts on board—yet. She was called the Gray Ghost because, like a phantom, she would appear in the enemy's sight, but she'd be gone before they could fire on her. She was fast, remember?

The troops aboard RMS *Queen Mary* did not experience the same comforts as her earlier passengers. Not only were the luxurious

interiors removed, but the ship had no air conditioning. Can you imagine? Because the ship had originally only traveled across the cold North Atlantic, there was no need for it. But now she was traveling through the hot and sticky South Pacific, Indian, and Mediterranean seas. And the lack of cooling systems and ventilation weren't just uncomfortable—they were deadly.

It is unknown exactly how many people died due to the extreme heat, but the number was high. Ah, maybe some of those people became the ghosts current visitors see? It's possible. Very, very possible. Hold on to that thought.

In 1942, the troop capacity of the ship was nearly doubled to 10,000, but she would carry more. In July 1943, she set a record with 15,740 armed troops and a crew of 943 for a grand total of 16,683 people on board. (That remains a record for the most people aboard a passenger ship ever.) It was crowded and uncomfortable, but everyone on *that* voyage made the five-day trip from New York to Scotland safely.

As the war continued, many American soldiers were injured, and eventually, they had to be returned to the United States. Once again, the *Queen Mary* underwent changes. This time, more than 1,000 double-tiered hospital beds were installed, along with a laboratory and new kitchens. More medical staff were added to the crew.

World War II ended in 1945, but the RMS *Queen Mary* still had duties to perform. Some of the people who had come to America six years earlier were ready to go back home to Europe. And there were still American troops to be brought back to the United States and families to be reunited.

In 1946, the ship's military service was officially done. The Gray Ghost had sailed more than 600,000 nautical miles during the war. She was never once fired upon, never had to fire her guns in battle, and never lost a single passenger to enemy action.

It was time for her to be restored to her original beauty and purpose. She had earned it!

The carpets, furniture, and artwork were returned to the ship. The mess halls became elegant dining rooms again. The bunks were removed, and beds placed back in the cabins. The ballrooms were prepared to host new

parties for happy, dancing passengers—live ones, as far as they knew.

The ship was also in need of structural and mechanical repairs. Thousands of workers labored day and night for ten months. In July 1947, she was completely refurbished and freshly painted in the Cunard colors of red, white, and black. The RMS *Queen Mary* once again set sail carrying passengers during peacetime.

All was well for a while, but by the late 1950s, the "Jet Age" of travel had arrived. People were flying more and more and sailing less and less. Plus, the cost of maintaining and operating large ocean liners was rising. Smaller, faster, ships were being built with newer, more-modern features. The *Queen Mary* was almost scrapped, but the City of Long Beach, California, purchased the historic vessel. It planned to permanently dock the ship as a floating museum and hotel.

After thirty-one years at sea, the RMS *Queen Mary* crossed the Atlantic one last time. She was tied to the dock in Long Beach, California, on December 9, 1967.

Then yet another transformation took place—this time to convert her from a passenger ship into a hotel and museum. Her structure also had to be reclassified. She still looked like a ship and remained afloat, but her official classification changed from a ship to a building. Crazy, right? Though people still refer to her as a ship—because she really kind of is— she is permanently moored and is no longer seaworthy.

The RMS *Queen Mary* has a long and fascinating history as a ship. She carried people to vacations, to new beginnings, to war, and back home again. There were plenty of joyful voyages, but also accidents. Tragedy struck more than once. In fact, the RMS *Queen Mary* is considered to be the most haunted ship in the world. So who are these restless souls that still lurk aboard? What happened to them? Why won't they leave? Let's find out.

MAIN FEED

R.M.S.

QUEEN MARY

The One and Only Captain John Treasure Jones

John Treasure Jones began working on English ships in 1921, when he was only fifteen. With a middle name like "Treasure," he probably could have become an infamous pirate. But Captain Jones did not take to the high seas to raid, pillage, and plunder. His legacy was built on caring for ships, guiding them and protecting them—passengers and cargo alike. More than forty years later, after an illustrious career (and distinguished service during World War II), Captain Jones became master of the greatest ship afloat, the queen of the queens: the RMS *Queen Mary*. It was December 1965. He was only her captain for two years, but he took great pride in the ship. You might even say she was a *treasure* to him. (See what I did there?) She was the last vessel he sailed aboard as captain, and John Treasure Jones was the last captain the RMS *Queen Mary* would ever know. And perhaps he never left.

Captain Jones did not die on the ship. In fact, he died almost thirty years later, far across the Atlantic, in the United Kingdom. But many people believe he has come back to keep watch over the *Queen Mary*. He is often seen—and heard—in different places on board.

And heard not just by visitors. Paranormal experts and ghost hunters have come aboard to record EVP, or electronic voice phenomena. EVP are sounds heard on electronic recordings that are believed to be spirit voices—GHOSTS TALKING—usually in single words or short phrases. What could be so important that a ghost would spend his energy trying to communicate with the living? Well, if that ghost is Captain Jones, it could be a warning or an order. Or perhaps he simply wants an explanation for some of the extreme alterations that have been made to his beloved ship, now that it's a hotel and a tourist attraction.

A hot spot for hearing Captain Jones's voice, either audibly or through EVP, is the propeller box. When the RMS *Queen Mary* was sailing, she had four giant propellers. After the ship was docked in Long Beach, three of her four propellers were removed. Then a huge hole was cut in the hull so visitors could view the remaining propeller. Some people think THIS is what brings Captain Jones to the propeller box; a gaping hole in his ship's hull would make any ship captain worried. Or angry. Or, at the very least, confused. I mean, the hull is supposed to keep water OUT. But no one can be sure if it is worry or fascination that brings him back to the propeller box or anywhere else on the ship. Whenever anyone tries to approach him, Captain Jones fades away before they can get close enough to ask.

It isn't only his image or his voice that alerts people to his presence. Captain Jones has another trick up his tailored uniform sleeve. As a living, breathing naval officer, he loved a good cigar. It seems he's carried the habit into the afterlife.

Rich tobacco smoke is frequently smelled near his favorite haunts, even though NO ONE is allowed to smoke in any room of the RMS *Queen Mary* today. Who would dare?

A daring captain taking a rest in his cabin just might. After all, smoking wasn't against the rules when he was alive. But no one has caught him in the act yet. And what would they do if they did? He'd probably disappear before they could do anything at all; vanish into thin air—like smoke.

The command center of a ship is called the bridge. There, you'll find the wheelhouse, the communications equipment, and the locations on deck where lookouts can spot hazards, such as icebergs in the distance. It was from the bridge of the RMS *Queen Mary* that Captain Jones and his navigation crew safely guided the ship on her voyages.

From the first time tourists were allowed aboard the reclassified ship in Long Beach, people have claimed to see a spectral, or ghostly, crew on the bridge. Throughout the years, guests have asked about the actors they have seen, only to find out there are no actors performing. If not actors or real, living people going through the duties of running a world-class ship, then what have the guests seen? You got it: ghosts.

There are reports of a captain standing at the wheel, staring out the front windows, as if he is still hard at work, guiding his greatest ship over the waves. Those who have seen this spirit describe him looking exactly as Captain Jones did when he first took command of the ship. Always a gentleman, he has been known to offer a polite nod to onlookers before he vanishes.

What remains of the captain's quarters is located just below the bridge, and Captain Jones has been seen resting in the small living room and office area. He has been heard humming in the bedroom. He's even been spotted in the pool area, but never out of uniform.

Perhaps someday he will explain why he's still there. Until then, paranormal investigators and curious guests will continue to listen for his voice and to watch for the devoted captain in his Cunard naval uniform.

Always a professional. Always on duty. It seems Captain Jones plans to command the RMS *Queen Mary* forever more.

CHAPTER 3

Little Jackie and Friends

The most popular ghost aboard the RMS *Queen Mary* is a playful girl named Jacqueline Torin. She is known as Little Jackie and is believed to be about five or six years old. The most remarkable thing about Little Jackie is the number of people who have heard her speak. She is definitely not shy. This girl has a lot to say!

Many spirits make themselves known through sounds, but Little Jackie speaks in very clear words and sometimes full sentences. This is pretty rare for a ghost. She might even answer direct questions and carry on a whole conversation—*if* she's in the mood.

A paranormal investigator named Peter James first met Little Jackie in the space that used to be the second-class pool in 1991. He heard her say, "Meet me in the other pool." In its heyday, the *Queen Mary* had two pools: one for first-class passengers and another for the rest of the passengers. Little Jackie is reported to have *drowned* in the second-class pool, so chances are she'd like to stay away from that one! That may be why she wanted to move their visit to the other pool. And once there, Little Jackie became very talkative. They talked for over ten minutes—and it was all caught on camera.

Like all children, Jackie giggles and plays, most often in the first-class pool area. That's clearly her favorite spot. Unlike the spirits who disappear or those angry ones who try to scare people away, Little Jackie seems to enjoy hanging out with the living.

She loves to play peek-a-boo with visitors from an upstairs balcony in the pool area. Once she's been spotted, she ducks away but quickly shows up in another part of the pool to keep the game going.

Jackie has also been heard greeting guests as they enter the Royal Theater. Maybe she likes having a job to do or maybe she just loves the theater, too. Maybe she thinks of herself as the star of the show. Why shouldn't she? She is the most famous of all the ship's ghosts!

Little Jackie has been heard from time to time asking for her mommy or her teddy, but she isn't always alone. She has a ghost friend named Sarah. Sarah is believed to be slightly older than Jackie, possibly as old as eight, but she may be able to make herself appear as a teenager. She is protective of Jackie, like an older sister would be.

Sometimes, when someone asks Little Jackie to speak to them, Sarah will answer instead with a very forceful, "No!" Sarah isn't as trusting as Jackie. She needs to get acquainted with people before she feels comfortable around them.

The two girls have been spotted together near the propeller box. Remember, there's a giant hole in the ship there. Who wouldn't

be interested in that? The sounds of running and laughing have been heard in the hallway outside the Royal Theater. The two girls have also been seen in the museum. The girls' spirits have been reported together all over the ship.

Little Jackie also has an older companion known as "the Lady in White." She gets her name from the lovely, long white dress she wears. This beautiful young woman is often seen dancing in the Queen's Salon to music that the living can't hear. This is the room where the rich and

famous would gather to dance the night away when the RMS *Queen Mary* was sailing across the North Atlantic. Sometimes she appears to be dancing alone, but other times, it appears she has an unseen partner.

Like Captain Jones, the Lady in White vanishes when anyone tries to approach her, but she has been known to offer a friendly smile before she disappears. The Lady in White has been sighted all over the ship, gliding across the dance floor, lingering near the piano, and gracefully moving up and down the staircases. Like other spirits on board, she can also be heard. She's kind but she doesn't giggle like Little Jackie. She sometimes speaks, but more often, she sings.

People have heard her singing in the hallway that leads to the first-class pool. Her voice is soothing and soft, and many times, a child can be heard humming along with her. Is it Little

Jackie? Could be. It is unclear if the Lady in White was related to Little Jackie while she was alive, or if she even knew her at all, but her gentle spirit seems to have adopted the little girl in the afterlife. Bringing comfort appears to be what the Lady in White enjoys most. She has been spotted in the isolation ward (basically an onboard hospital), visiting the patients who never got well.

The Lady in White also has a protective side. When she's been spotted near the propeller box, it is believed she is looking out for Little Jackie and Sarah to make sure the girls don't get hurt. Those girls love to run!

With Sarah and the Lady in White protecting and comforting her, Little Jackie has at least two great spirits keeping her company. And really, who *wouldn't* want to spend their afterlife playing and wandering—and spooking guests—on a glorious ship?

ISOLATION WARD

Sir Winston Churchill and the Dude

Dude. WINSTON CHURCHILL HAUNTS THE *QUEEN MARY*. If you don't know who Winston Churchill is, look him up. He was the prime minister of the UK during World War II and is an extremely important character in world history. He didn't die aboard RMS *Queen Mary*, but he did travel aboard quite a bit. And because he was such an important world figure, he always sailed under a code name. It was especially important during the war to keep his presence aboard the ship secret. So you won't see "Winston Churchill" in any of the passenger logs. But you will see someone by the name of Colonel Warden. (Pssst. That was his code name.) Good old Winston not only had a private suite, but also a private office on the Promenade Deck of the *Queen Mary*. The desk he used while he was on board during the war is located in the Churchill Suite today. It is said he spent a lot of time in his office and suite, making important decisions and weighing the consequences.

Prime Minister Churchill knew the decision to send his countrymen into battle was a tough one and would cause thousands of deaths. He knew not everyone would agree with his actions. Some people speculate that his spirit remains on board because he never stopped worrying about his wartime decisions.

Today, the space that used to be his office is a store. Churchill has been seen standing by the fireplace that was, at one time, directly behind his desk. Maybe he's wondering who moved all that stuff into his office. How is he supposed to get any work done in a store?

Like Captain Jones, Winston Churchill's spirit is also connected to the smell of cigar smoke. (Churchill was famously fond of cigars.) But there's a difference. Ghost hunters attribute some smoke to Churchill because they smell it in the areas that the prime minister stayed in or visited frequently. He had a favorite brand of cigars that was sold onboard.

Churchill's cigar smoke is often noticed at the suite that bears his name. And the sounds of pacing footsteps and worried mumbling have been heard in the Churchill Suite, even when no guest was staying in the room. The same smoke is noticeable in and around the space that was his office. No guest can be seen breaking the current no smoking rule when the smell arrives. It must be Colonel Warden, lighting up another cigar.

Sir Winston's, a restaurant at the rear of the ship, is named for him. It is the fanciest restaurant on board. And, you guessed it, Churchill's smoke can be smelled there, too. Mostly in the bar area.

Guests have even complained to the staff about the strong odor of the cigar smoke at the restaurant. But like everywhere else onboard, no living guests can ever be found smoking when the smell is detected. Maybe the cigar smoke in Sir Winston's shows that the prime minister doesn't spend all his time on board worrying in his old office. Maybe he's enjoying the social atmosphere and cocktails at the restaurant. Or maybe he is simply making sure the restaurant is living up to his name.

Winston Churchill isn't the only spirit who likes to spend his time in Sir Winston's. The restaurant frequently plays host to a spirit known as "the Dude." His true identity remains a mystery, but he is a ghost of distinction. The Dude appears in a top hat and a tailcoat; he is a man of great style. He probably went to fancy restaurants with fine menus when he was alive, too. It is believed he was a wealthy passenger who sailed first class on the RMS *Queen Mary*.

The Dude prefers the bar area of Sir Winston's restaurant. He will vanish before anyone can interact with him, but he does like to be noticed. Even better, this well-dressed ghost likes to pull pranks on people, surprising them for his own amusement.

There are many reports of him approaching guests from behind and clearing his throat until they turn and see him, at which point he disappears. He either vanishes into thin air or walks right through the wall that leads to the men's restroom. Dude, seriously?

Some guests must wonder if they imagined him. After all, a man walking through a solid wall doesn't happen every day.

The Dude doesn't always seek attention. Sometimes he sits or stands alone, quietly watching the guests with a smile on his face. His slicked-back hair is always perfectly in place. Like most of the spirits on board, the Dude has never threatened or harmed anyone. He seems content to admire the living folks who wander into the restaurant he now calls home.

Perhaps the Dude dined with Colonel Warden when they were both alive. They might've been friends. Or maybe their paths never crossed at all until their spirits found their way to Sir Winston's bar.

Do they sometimes enjoy a nice meal and a cigar together in the afterlife? Are they friends or strangers, keeping an eye on each other?

Only Winston Churchill and the Dude know for sure.

John Pedder and Unlucky Door Number 13

John Pedder was only eighteen in 1966, when he worked aboard the RMS *Queen Mary* down in the engine room. For many young men in England at that time, a chance to work for the Cunard company was a dream come true. (Remember: Cunard owned and operated the *Queen Mary*.) It meant a long and profitable career lay ahead. Unfortunately for Pedder, a reckless choice would cut his career short.

The engine room of a ship is a dangerous place. On the *Queen Mary*, it is located at the center of the ship well below the water line. When the ship was sailing, there were huge, moving engine parts and tremendous heat from the boilers and generators. Shifts were long, and the job duties themselves could be boring. It was difficult to work in such exhausting conditions.

When the engine crew got bored, they'd create ways to entertain themselves. Some of the ideas the younger men came up with were just stupid. They were often risky and seriously unsafe. One of these bad ideas would cost young John Pedder his life.

The *Queen Mary* was equipped with watertight doors that could be closed automatically in the event of flooding (due to an accident or bad weather). These doors had a tight seal that would keep the compartments dry. They were meant to keep people and equipment safe.

Because the watertight doors were a safety feature, the captain sometimes called a drill—a test to be sure they were working properly. An alarm would alert the crew that a drill was about to begin. The doors closed quickly, allowing only a brief time for everyone to get on the right side of them.

Some of the men started a game to test the time limits of the door mechanism—and the limits of their courage. They would wait and run through the doors at the LAST possible second. Whoever waited the longest was clearly the bravest, so each time, the crew would wait longer and longer. Then one day, John Pedder waited a second too long. He was crushed by watertight door Number 13, and killed instantly.

John Pedder has haunted the shaft near door Number 13 ever since. People often hear a man whispering around them in that area. He is known to ignore men but to pay special attention to women. He apparently likes to flirt. Young John Pedder is believed to be capable of stroking women's hair and tickling their ears. He isn't too shy to get close. Some have even reported feeling his breath on their cheeks. (Creepy.)

Folks near the engine room have also reported the sounds of chains and gears moving, as well as knocking noises that move from one part of the engine room to another when anyone approaches. But John Pedder may prefer to make himself known with more than touches and sounds. Several people have reported seeing a young man riding up with them in the elevator. They describe the man as being dressed in an engineer's uniform. But the hotel reports that there is no employee assigned to the elevator, and if there were, they certainly wouldn't be wearing an engine room uniform from the1960s. Could these people be sharing the elevator with the gutsy ghost of young John Pedder as he arrives for his next shift? Maybe he rides the elevator to be sure everyone is safe. Perhaps the elevator doors remind him of his own fate? Is he there to be sure everyone gets on and off before the doors crush them? If you ever visit, perhaps you'll get the chance to ask him.

Fedora Dude, a Dude of a Different Type

While most of the ghosts on the RMS *Queen Mary* don't seem to have any sinister intentions at all, there is one who leaves people feeling uneasy. Like the ghost known only as the Dude, the spirit known as "Fedora Dude" is also well dressed, but in a different style. He gets his name from his bright yellow fedora. He wears it with a yellowish-tan zoot suit, a much less formal look than the top hat and tailcoat worn by the Dude and from a different time. A zoot suit had a loose-fitting jacket with big shoulder pads. It was a casual look from the 1940s. Paired with a fedora, it's clear Fedora Dude hails from that era. Also like the Dude, Fedora Dude's real identity is unknown. But very much *unlike* the charming appearance of the Dude, Fedora Dude looks terrifying. He is extremely tall with hollow, yellow eyes and rotten teeth.

Fedora Dude is bold. He does not disappear as soon as he is seen. He is most often spotted in the lobby area of the hotel and is known to smirk at guests while he passes close by, as if he knows a secret about them. Once he has moved past the guests, he turns down a hallway out of view.

If anyone tries to follow him, by the time they reach the hallway, the fedora-wearing specter will have moved so far away so fast, it doesn't make sense. He will turn back, smile, and then fade away.

Fedora Dude likes to offer his chilling smirk and show his menacing smile, but he does not appear to want to engage with guests in any other way. He seems to enjoys making guests nervous and afraid. Maybe it makes him feel powerful to make the living feel suspicious and fearful. Jerk.

This fully formed specter with the yellow hat, yellow suit, and yellow eyes has been seen all over the public areas of the ship at all hours of the day and night.

Fedora Dude never rests. Those who've met him up close probably have a little trouble sleeping after they've felt his ominous, rotten grin cast down upon them. Thank goodness he can't breathe anymore, because his ghastly breath would probably sink the ship!

Jack and Terrance, Reporting for Duty

Jack and Terrance are spirits who consistently show up together. They appear to be soldiers, and it is believed they may have died during the ship's Gray Ghost era of World War II.

As mentioned before, the *Queen Mary* was designed without air conditioning. That wasn't a feature she would need traveling the cold north Atlantic route, but when she began transporting soldiers across the Indian Ocean and the Mediterranean Sea, the extreme heat on board actually killed people. Jack and Terrance may have been among those who died due to the unbearable temperatures.

If a ghost is going to announce its arrival with a temperature change—which many do—it is almost always with a DROP in temperature. People will report they get a sudden chill or feel a cold draft that makes no sense considering the comfortable temperature everywhere else. But not with Jack and Terrance. Intense heat usually accompanies these two. This unusual temperature detail makes it seem likely that heat was indeed a factor in their deaths.

Because these two always show up together, most think that they were friends and that they may have died at or around the same time. Jack and Terrance inhabit the first-class pool area. People often report hearing them state their names clearly, as if they are trying to make it obvious that they are still here.

The duo is pretty playful. Guests report feeling a tug on their clothes when Jack and Terrance are around, as if the soldiers are trying to get their attention. But no one has ever reported getting hurt or feeling threatened by them.

Did Jack and Terrance ever serve in battle? Did their (maybe) heat-related deaths happen during war? We may never know. Their full identities have not been confirmed. Maybe someday we will know who they were and if they were sailing into battle or back home again.

In the meantime, hopefully, these soldiers are enjoying some rest and relaxation and their memories of taking a nice cold dip in the pool.

MAIN FEED

R.M.S.

QUEEN MARY

CHAPTER 8

William Eric Stark, Who Would be a Good Host Even if it Killed Him

Senior Second Officer William Eric Stark was getting off duty when the ship's captain asked a favor of him. The captain wanted Officer Stark to entertain a couple of new crew officers, to try to make them feel welcome. Stark found the new officers and invited them to stop by his cabin later.

After hurrying back to his quarters, Officer Stark called for a steward and asked him to get a bottle of gin. The steward went into another cabin close by to quickly look for a bottle of gin. He thought it was great luck that he found one so easily, and he took it back to Officer Stark's cabin right away.

What the steward didn't realize was that the man in the other cabin had already drunk all the gin that had been in the bottle. He had refilled the bottle with a strong cleaning liquid so it didn't LOOK empty. But he never intended anyone to drink it—that would be deadly.

Officer Stark poured himself a drink from the bottle, added lime juice, and waited for his guests. When the new crew members arrived, they quickly realized that what Stark had poured them was *not* gin. Stark was surprised and embarrassed, but otherwise fine. He laughed it off and went to find a real bottle of gin.

It wasn't until the next day that Officer Stark became violently ill. He was taken to the medical ward, but there was nothing the doctor could do to save him. He died.

Stark's spirit has been seen roaming the Promenade Deck. He is described as wandering around like he is dazed or confused. He has also been seen in and around the captain's quarters. Some believe he is searching for the captain of the watch, the man who directed him to entertain the new officers. Stark might want to apologize for accidentally serving the men poison. Or perhaps he is angry because he agreed to do the captain a favor in the first place. Maybe he's searching for the steward who brought him a bottle of poison instead of gin.

The only thing that seems certain is Officer Stark took his last drink aboard the RMS *Queen Mary*.

John Henry's Work is Never Done

Imagine being a performer, thrilled to be part of one of the wonderful productions that the *Queen Mary* puts on to entertain guests. And not just any guests! You're in Los Angeles, after all. Famous actors and directors and producers could be aboard. This could be your big break or just a chance to do what you love on stage.

But then, on your first night, you're getting ready for the show. You're in your dressing room. History tells you that this space was once one of the ship's generator rooms but was later transformed into a dressing room. You're not quite sure what a generator room was used for, but you definitely hear knocking sounds. And some banging. Is there construction going on?

You look outside the room. Nothing. No workmen, no hammers. There's a wooden walkway that goes past the dressing area. You hear whispers, but you don't see anyone. What is going ON?

Then you see him: a figure, crouched on a stairwell that leads up to a platform. "Hello?" you call, as bravely as you can. The figure turns back and looks at you. "Hello!" you say again. And then all of a sudden HE'S GONE. Just . . . gone.

Okay, this is nuts, right? I mean, you heard the *Queen Mary* was haunted but none of that was really *true*, right?

You go back to your dressing room and shake it off. You finish getting ready when you notice the square hole in the ceiling of the room. Had that always been there? Wait, is there someone up there? You look away but watch the reflection in the mirror. And then you see them. The glowing eyes. Looking right. At. You.

In a burst of courage you didn't know you had, you grab a flashlight and shine it right were the glowing eyes were! But again, they're gone. They've retreated into the ceiling. THIS IS INSANE.

You grab your stuff and run, looking for another place to get ready. Or maybe you should leave? But you're due on stage in a few minutes!

Well, you stuck around. You made it through your performance, and it was a great night.

Back in the creepy, haunted dressing room, you're talking to a few of the performers who've been working on the ship a lot longer than you have. You know it sounds absolutely crazy, but you mention the whispers, the banging, the crouched figure, the *eyes*.

"Oh yeah," they tell you. "That's John Henry."

"He has a name?!"

"Sure. They think he was probably a welder or a boiler room worker who died while on the job. Some people say he may have been one of the workers during the construction of the ship, back in the 1930s. His spirit resides around here and only here. He's never seen anywhere else on the ship."

"Yeah, folks think he's still here because he never finished the job he was supposed to do. Oh, and he seems to really only like women. You'll hear his voice telling men to get out. Male actors, and even guests in the area, will feel something pulling and pushing on them, trying to get them to leave. To be honest, a lot of actors quit on the spot when John Henry's around. You've got some guts for sticking around."

So it's true. The boat is haunted. You've seen it firsthand. And you're pretty sure it's not going to get better. So what do you do? Come back tomorrow night for another performance? Or abandon ship?

ISOLATION WARD

Daniel, the Blue Boy

Daniel is only five or six years old, and he is often called "the Blue Boy." He doesn't have blue skin or blue hair, but he is always seen wearing distinctive blue clothes that appear to be from the Edwardian era. That's just fancy for some time around 1900–1912 (named for the British king at the time, Edward VII).

This little boy is most frequently seen wandering on the Promenade Deck and around the staircase in the shopping area of the ship. He has also been spotted in the Observation Bar and other areas of the upper level.

Sounds captured on EVP indicate he is looking for his parents. No one knows how he got away from them, but he definitely wants to find them.

Edwardian fashion went out of style around 1914, but construction on the RMS *Queen Mary* didn't begin until sixteen years later in 1930. Many people believe that this child could have been from a poor immigrant family, wearing hand-me-downs. His family may not have been able to afford new clothing. Remember that the ship had three classes of tickets. So despite her beauty and opulence, many immigrants sailed to America aboard the *Queen Mary*. Then again, maybe the blue clothes weren't the boy's regular clothes after all. Maybe he was wearing a costume or playing dress-up. Someday, this boy in blue might be able to provide more information. Until then, he continues to play and wander the ship, looking for his parents.

David and Sarah, Parents Always

While Little Jackie and Daniel are believed to be looking for their parents, David and Sarah are adult spirits who may be looking for their children. They are always seen together, and while they're not hostile or frightening, they don't wish to be bothered by anyone who can't help them in their quest.

The pair are often seen at the first-class pool, which is not surprising. Kids LOVE pools!

It's the first stop I'd look if my kids ran off on a cruise ship, amiright?

David and Sarah are also seen at Sir Winston's restaurant. They often seem to have a confused or curious look on their faces. Do they have questions to ask of the guests or the staff? Are they actually looking for their children (or are they waiting for a table to open up so they can get dinner)?

When approached by guests, the two will usually disappear. But they have been known to respond to paranormal investigators who address them by name. They've even answered investigators' questions!

But still, no one knows exactly who David and Sarah are—or were. Nor do we know who their children are—or were. Some speculate that Daniel or Little Jackie may be the kids in question. But if they were, don't you think they'd have found their parents by now? I mean, if the living can find all these ghosts running (floating?) around the boat, wouldn't the spirits reunite on their own? And if they did, then they'd be at peace and disappear forever. So the general thought is that David and Sarah will continue to search for what they hold most dear.

Shadow People and Balls of Light

Ever catch a shadow from the corner of your eye, turn around, and find nothing there? Weird, right? Well, that probably *won't* happen if you see one of "the Shadow People" on the RMS *Queen Mary*. Meaning, they won't disappear when you turn your head to see them. They don't seem to mind if you notice their forms moving about. But you'll never see their faces.

Because the Shadow People are too mysterious, too dark. Only shapes. Shadows.

Shadow People have been seen all over the ship at all hours. No one is exactly sure what they are. Some people describe them as having an almost smoky appearance. Others say they look like oil on water. Some people see a shimmering aura around them.

They are different heights and weights just like real people. But they most definitely are not real people. There are many theories about the Shadow People. Are they from another dimension? Are they simply another form of ghosts? Could they be demons?

No one has ever been able to get close enough to see more specific details. They keep their distance, remaining shadowy and secretive. People walking in the ship's long hallways have reported seeing one of the dark figures farther along, standing still as if staring back at them. Some have even captured images of them and posted them online.

Sometimes the beings vanish into thin air, and other times they disappear through the walls. But whoever witnesses one is left with a creepy feeling that something bad may be about to happen.

We may never know exactly what these specters are, but it is certain they exist and visit the RMS *Queen Mary* often. They may be drawn to the ship's history or the number of deaths that occurred on board.

On the lighter side of *Queen Mary*'s MANY unexplained sightings are the balls of light. These are different from what paranormal fans usually referred to as orbs. Orbs are bright circles that show up on digital photographs and often have a logical explanation. The balls of light spotted aboard the ship are visible to the human eye with no cameras or special equipment needed. Ranging in size from a grape all the way up to a softball, they are often blue but have been reported in colors across the spectrum.

The balls of light have been seen traveling in a straight line with a slight up-and-down wobble. They produce their own glow and can be seen cruising along in total darkness, not trying to hide or dim their brightness when people are around. They also show up in photographs, but they do not appear flat like orbs. There is depth and dimension to them that makes them look solid.

Down in the cargo hold, people have witnessed lights that zoomed all around. At other times, they have appeared still, like stars up near the ceiling.

No one is sure what these balls of light are or why they are there. Of course, some believe they could be spirits. If so, some estimate that there could be more than six-hundred spirits on board the ship. Perhaps they can't all appear in a recognizable human form or shape.

CHAPTER 13

First-Class Pool: Vortex and Home to a Grouch (and a cat!)

A *vortex* is defined as a swirling mass of air or liquid that creates an open area in the center. That area in the center can pull things toward it, like a vacuum. In water, it's a whirlpool. Some people believe the first-class pool area on the RMS *Queen Mary* is actually a vortex that allows spirits to cross between our world and another realm. While the first-class pool no longer holds water today, it *did* for a while once the ship was docked in Long Beach. And it was definitely a fully functioning pool while the ship was still sailing.

Regardless if there's water involved, there is SOMETHING about the first-class pool that provides the portal, or passageway, for the ship's spirits. It also makes it the ultimate location for detecting spirits as they come and go. Because of this, the area is a favorite with paranormal investigators. It's actually the most visited part of the ship. This is where people come to try to find Little Jackie and her friends. They gather around the pool with toys, candy, and stuffed animals. Sometimes they sing "Ring Around the Rosie" to get her to come out and play with them. (Sometimes it works!)

It is believed the exact spot of the vortex that serves as a portal for the ghosts is located in the narrow hallway between the changing closets. (They're not really closets. More like bathroom stalls, but for changing into and out of your bathing suit.) Three stalls back from the port, or left, side is where you want to be. It is said that if you stand in that spot, you will feel the hair on your arms or on the back of your neck stand up. Or you may get goosebumps. You might even start to feel dizzy.

Have you ever felt as if you were being watched? That's how some people feel near this spot. Their heart rate speeds up, and they have a strong urge to RUN from the cramped space. People investigating in the area have heard the whispers of a little girl and a British woman. They have seen a shadowy man who watches them and then vanishes.

There are even reports of a cat in this area—a ghost cat! The ghost cat prances by as people sit in the changing stalls and has even been known to brush up against a guest every now and then.

It acts just like a living cat and has been seen by whole groups of people at once. This spirited feline doesn't mind being admired. He seems to want to say, "What are you looking at? Never seen a ghost cat before?"

There's another space in the pool room that also causes people to experience intense feelings and strange sensations, but there is no cute cat there, no playful Little Jackie. This dark and eerie place has freaked out guests and investigators alike. It is a small room directly under the staircase at the front of the pool. It is accessed by a narrow, extremely low hallway—so low, in fact, that most people have to stoop to enter the room itself.

This is the home of "Grumpy the Growling Ghost." He earned his nickname because he growls at people when they get near. Obviously, he wants to be left alone. Totally and completely alone.

Many people have heard him growling as they approached the small room, and some have seen glowing eyes staring back at them from the dark. They don't have to wonder if they're being watched. They know for sure.

Grumpy sometimes leaves his hiding place under the stairs and moves close to a guest. He's been known to growl right up against someone's ear, so close the visitor can feel their earlobe vibrate.

Investigators have heard a loud growl interrupt the Lady in White while she sings and even Little Jackie while she hums, causing the little girl to scream in terror. No one is sure why Grumpy dislikes the singing and humming. If his outbursts are intended to torment

Little Jackie, his reason for that is a mystery, too. Many times, investigators have conducted an EVP session in Grumpy's area when they get an overwhelming sense of fear or dread. The uneasy feeling will get worse and worse until they can't take it anymore and they feel forced to run for their lives. Grumpy's space may be tiny, but the scare is enormous.

Many people have smelled cigar smoke in Grumpy's area, and it is similar to the smoky scent connected to Captain Jones. Some people wonder if Captain Jones and Grumpy may actually be the same spirit.

But Grumpy the Growling Ghost does not behave like a dignified ship's captain. Captain Jones was always professional and a gentleman when he lived, and his spirit has behaved the same way ever since. It's possible Captain Jones and Grumpy enjoyed the same cigars in life, but it is unlikely that they are the same spirit.

But *why* is Grumpy so darn grumpy? Some stories suggest that he was a passenger who killed someone while he was on board. Who did he kill? And why? Those stories are lost to history.

But if he *did* kill someone on board, then Grumpy might be sticking around because he is afraid of what awaits him on the other side. Maybe this is why he growls if anyone gets too close to him. It is just one theory about Grumpy, and not everyone believes it. But people do agree that Grumpy is pretty nasty and is best avoided.

The living may not always like being near the vortex, but as long as the spirits continue to appear, people will come to see them. Investigators will come back again and again to try to solve the mysteries of the first-class pool.

More Hot Spots for Sighting Cool Ghosts

The first-class pool is a major hot spot for ghost-sightings on the RMS *Queen Mary*, but there are others. Over the years, people have argued about which section of the ship might be the *most* haunted. Many paranormal investigators will say the first-class pool area is the most active. But that's also the first place people check for Little Jackie—the boat's most popular ghost. So is that really the most active spot? Or just the spot more people go to find their favorite ghost? With such a high population of spirits on board, it only makes sense that they would move all around the historic ship. So, when they're not coming and going through the vortex in the pool area or hanging out in some of the areas we've already visited, where else can the ghosts be found?

Room B-474

Some stories claim room B-340 is the most haunted guest room. Stories tell of a whole family who died in this hotel room. Ghostly moans come out of thin air in the middle of the night in this room, doors open and close on their own, and water faucets in the bathroom turn on and off without anyone touching them.

One of the most common mischievous occurrences in the room is the covers being moved after the bed is made. The covers have even been known to fly off of sleeping guests in the middle of the night, as if yanked off by a ghost.

Now, all these occurrences have occurred, but not in room B-340.

The truth is room B-340 has never actually been a hotel room. The real room associated with the original stories is room B-474. Why the confusion?

Back in the day, the ship ran a Ghosts and Legends tour (much like the ghost tours of today) to show off the ghostliness of the ship. With guests actually staying in the very haunted room B-474, the tour couldn't really take other visitors to the room. (You wouldn't like it if strangers trotted through your hotel room while on vacation, would you?) So instead, the ship converted an unused area to room B-340 and brought the tour through there (all the while telling the tales of B-474). There may indeed be spirits haunting the space that became room B-340 for the tour, but room B-474 is the real room featured in the original story, the one where a whole family died in their cabin.

Guests have reported many incidents of ghostly encounters in room B-474 ever since the hotel opened. People have heard sounds of a man and woman arguing when there was no one staying in the room. Guests of B-474 have felt strange cool breezes and someone standing over them, watching them. Some guests have even reported feeling as though someone was trying to choke them! Are these members of the deceased family? Are they angry? Just bored? No one knows.

It seems that staying in room B-474 might be a great choice for those who aren't afraid to meet a ghost, possibly even an angry one. But the easily frightened might want to enjoy the tales of the most haunted room on the ship from less active quarters, where they can sleep soundly without fear of anyone jerking their covers away in the middle of the night.

THE ISOLATION WARD

The Isolation Ward, located on B Deck, is a hot spot for paranormal activity. While the ship was in service, this area functioned as a hospital. It was also a disease control room to keep patients from spreading any illnesses to other passengers.

In the early career of the RMS *Queen Mary*, the science about how infections or diseases worked and spread was not as advanced or well-known as it is today. Whenever a passenger got sick and it was suspected they might be contagious, they were placed in the Isolation Ward to protect the other passengers and the crew.

Stowaways, or people who were found to have snuck on board without a ticket, were often kept there as well. And anyone who was kind of a jerk and behaved in a dangerous manner was also placed in the Isolation Ward. They had to keep everyone else on the boat safe. The crew and first-class passengers had their own medical ward, but second-class and third-class passengers had only the Isolation Ward for medical care. And during World War II, the Isolation Ward was where they kept any sick prisoners of war while they were being transported on the RMS *Queen Mary*.

Over the years, guests have reported seeing ghostly doctors moving in the different rooms of the ward. And they have seen men and women lying in the bunks that are now behind a glass wall. Some have seen a nurse taking care of unseen patients. Many believe that nurse may have died while on board.

The Lady in White has been seen in the ward often. Because of her kind nature, people believe she comes to visit and bring cheer to the patients who are still there.

People have heard voices in this area speaking in various languages, including German and Italian. These spirits could be prisoners of war who didn't survive their trip.

Beyond the Isolation Ward, there was a morgue set up during World War II. (You know what a morgue is, right? A place to store dead bodies.) This area is off limits during most of the year. But during Halloween, the boat hires actors for a special spooky event for tourists. Some actors have refused to work in the morgue area because of their experiences with spirits there. They are convinced there is

a paranormal energy there that is not part of their act.

But the ghostly medical staff remains devoted to their jobs. As long as apparitions of patients and the sounds of their sickly moans continue to appear, the doctors and nurses will perform their duties in the Isolation Ward.

THE ROYAL THEATER

The Royal Theater is located directly across the hall from the propeller box, in the area where the second-class pool used to be. It is where Little Jackie was first discovered, which is not surprising, as she reportedly drowned in the second-class pool. Perhaps this is why she is still seen and heard in the area. Regardless, she does love to hang out here, in and around the Royal Theater.

Ghostly reports from this area include

the sound of mysterious music playing and shadows moving around. Sometimes the shadows are seen sitting in the audience as if they are watching a show, even when there is none taking place—as far as living eyes can see.

Some of the spirits in the theater are recognizable. Captain Jones has been heard in the area outside the theater (near the propeller box). The Lady in White has been heard and seen in the area. Grumpy has even been heard growling about now and then.

A living cat never gets to go to the theater, but the *Queen Mary*'s ghost cat does! Why wouldn't it? The chance to explore between the seats, dart down the aisles, and romp around on stage (in its afterlife) must be fun for a cat. The Royal Theater is a gathering spot for entertainment among the ship's resident spirits, who sometimes take their seats to enjoy a show that's just for them.

THE PROMENADE DECK

Almost all passenger ships have a promenade deck. It's an upper deck with a lot of outdoor space, usually running the whole length of the ship. It gives passengers the chance to walk around outside, or promenade (which is just an old-timey word for "take a leisurely walk, either for pleasure or to be seen"). The Promenade Deck on the *Queen Mary* was a popular spot for passengers to people watch and to spot the celebrities and wealthy passengers who were aboard. At any given time, there were travelers strolling up and down the polished deck or sitting in the lounge chairs in one of the many sitting rooms, garden rooms, or libraries.

This was also where the bustling Piccadilly Square shopping area was located. The Observation Bar at the front of the Promenade Deck was a great place for guests to listen to music and relax. The Queen's Salon was on this deck as well, and it was often filled with the sounds of bands playing or comedians telling jokes. The Promenade Deck truly was the hub of social activity on the RMS *Queen Mary*.

Some of the former passengers and crew still wander the wooden deck in search of the joyous times they once had there. In addition to dancing in the Queen's Salon, the Lady in White has also been seen walking along the deck, as if she doesn't have a care in the world. This lovely lady has been spotted in the Observation Bar, Promenade Café, and other areas on the deck as well.

Officer Stark (remember him? He was the guy who drank cleaning solution instead of gin) is often seen here. Guests hoping to see him should keep their eyes open *everywhere* on the Promenade Deck. But beware! He might not be too steady on his feet. He's been poisoned, after all.

Captain Jones is another crew member who is often seen on the deck. He carries himself with an unmistakable authority that makes it clear he is the master of the ship, keeping watch, making sure all is well.

This deck is where the mysterious figures known as the Shadow People are commonly seen. These dark, faceless shapes may keep their distance but they're still there, watching the living.

The Promenade Deck is—and was—a popular spot with guests and passengers. It remains a favorite haunt for many of their spirits, who can be seen strolling along as if they are still enjoying their transatlantic voyage.

THE FORWARD CARGO HOLD

The forward cargo hold is definitely one of the most haunted sections of the ship. This area in the way bottom of the ship, all the way at the front, is now off-limits to visitors, but it remains a place that investigators hope to visit.

Even some of those who were lucky enough to explore it many times in the past would like to go back. What could be so interesting down there, deep in the dark belly of the ship?

During World War II, this space was often overcrowded with prisoners of war who were being sent to the United States. The prisoners were assigned a bunk that they had to share with one or more fellow prisoners. They had to take turns and sleep in shifts, which meant no one got much rest. The cargo hold was a rough, cold, damp, and very dark place. It must have felt like being trapped in a dungeon.

Because of these awful conditions, many prisoners of war died before they reached their destination. Some of them died due to illnesses like pneumonia, while others suffered fatal injuries when violent weather created rough seas. In December 1942, the *Queen Mary* was struck by an enormous rogue wave and came terrifyingly close to capsizing. Soldiers, crew, and prisoners were thrown around the ship, slamming into walls, ceilings, and decks. Thousands were injured. On the deck above is the Isolation Ward, where the prisoners went for medical attention. It wasn't as nice as the medical ward that was on the ship during peacetime, but doctors and nurses were there to treat the prisoners' illnesses and injuries as best they could. And you remember what's next to the Isolation Ward, right? The temporary morgue.

Maybe that's why visitors and investigators have noticed a lot of paranormal activity in this area. Most commonly reported is the voice of a British woman down near the cargo hold and on the decks above it. Some believe she may have been a nurse who died due to a storm tossing the ship on the waves. Was she a victim of the rogue wave? We don't know.

One of the worst disasters involving the RMS *Queen Mary* occurred on October 2, 1942. The ship was being escorted by a much smaller boat called the HMS *Curacoa* when the ocean liner collided with it. The force of the crash SPLIT the smaller vessel in half! More than 330 soldiers aboard the *Curacoa* were lost. The collision remains one of the worst accidents in British maritime history. The forward cargo hold on the *Queen Mary* is very close to the spot where the collision occurred.

People have claimed to hear the sound of rushing water spilling into the ship, along with the sounds of men screaming in this area. Tour guides always try to calm and reassure the guests when this happens. But the sounds are so vivid, some guests have fled because they were convinced the ship was about to sink. Investigators believe that the tragedy of the *Curacoa* is the source of these alarming sounds.

Visitors have also heard voices speaking in different languages—mostly German and Italian—near the forward cargo hold. Some can be heard without the aid of equipment, but many more have been captured as EVP. Some of the voices have been caught talking about the paranormal investigators themselves! The voices are wondering who the investigators are and why they are there bothering the spirits. What do they want? The most curious of the voices speaks with a British accent. Many believe these talkative and inquisitive spirits may be those of the lost *Curacoa* crew members.

There is also lots of strange activity involving light in the cargo hold. The balls of light mentioned earlier are often seen in there, as well as sparks falling from the ceiling as if someone is welding. The sparks will fall for a few moments and then simply vanish.

With all the suffering and death that took place in this area of the hull, it's no wonder that it would be filled with restless souls. Here, and in so many other places on board the RMS *Queen Mary*, spirits seem to outnumber the living. And they may never leave.

The RMS *Queen Mary* is more than just a ship, a hotel, a museum, and a tourist attraction. She is history itself and, quite possibly, the most haunted place you could ever visit.

Shelli Timmons writes for kids of all ages. After many years working with numbers, she realized she liked letters a whole lot more, so she stepped away from the world of finance and entered the realm of stories. She loves old houses and buildings, and is always open to sharing space with a ghost or two. She currently lives in Central Texas in a house much newer than she'd prefer, with an equal number of people and dogs.

Check out some of the other Spooky America titles available now!

Spooky America was adapted from the creeptastic Haunted America series for adults. Haunted America explores historical haunts in cities and regions across America. Here's more from the original *Ghosts of the Queen Mary* authors Brian Clune with Bob Davis:

www.parainvestigations.com
www.queenmaryshadows.com